I believe in my heart as adults if we truly want to make God smile we should pray to him at all times in order to establish a strong relationship with him.

But if you want to see him really shine upon us it's important for us to teach our children how to pray and instill in them the importance of prayer as well as helping them to trust and rely on God because God is the only one that every man woman and child should be truly committed to.

God bless the parents, Grandparents and anyone who takes time to pray for and with our young children.

1.

As the Robinson family awakes on this beautiful morning a little voice soft and gentle says good morining mommy and daddy. Mommy and daddy reply good morining Victoria we love you and Victoria in return says love you and as she does every morning she jumps into the bed with her parents.

There they cuddle up together and Dad begins to say the morining prayer.

Father God we thank you for protecting us through out the night We thank you for your love, guidance, wisdom and forgiveness, please continue to protect us and direct us on how we should walk and instruct us on how to live peacefully with one another and amongst our neighbors and please protect us from our enemies as we go through the day in the name of Jesus we pray and ask these things Amen.

2.

Victoria asks her parents what is an enemy, so Victoria's mother explains an enemy is a person who has hate toward other people and intend to harm another person. Dad and mom talk to Victoria about being loving and kind to everyone because it is how God wants us to be. Although there are mean spirited people in the world if we see ourselves as Gods children and true Christians we must treat each other with respect and show kindness no matter what your faith or race may be being nice to people is a wonderful thing to do.

3.

To God Be the Glory

Never stop praising God

Never lose Faith in God

God hears your prayers and he will answer them

Always give thanks and praise God for giving your life and blessing you for what you have.

4.

As the Robinson family gather in the kitchen to have breakfast Victoria's Dad makes her favorite which is pancakes, eggs and turkey bacon the family converses about the plans for the day while Victoria's mother sets the table.

The family sits and joins hands and pray over the breakfast that Dad has prepared.

God, we thank you for this food for rest and home and all things good we thank you for blessing us to be a happy loving family and standing strong together through critical times and we are grateful for all the good times that you bless us with but we are most thankful for your everlasting love, in Jesus name we pray Amen.

5.

Teaching children to have faith in God makes God very happy

Parents should always teach their children how to pray and keep faith in God

When parents love their children with all their heart and educate their children about God, God is also pleased with the parents and will bless the entire family with his everlasting love.

6.

Jesus is the true meaning of Love and Peace

Let us appreciate the gift that Jesus gave us

By living in harmony with one another.

7.

On Sunday's Victoria and her parents attend church where they can worship with friends and family.

Victoria enjoys sitting with her parents in church having fun giving thanks to God.

8.

After church on Sundays the family gets together for a delicious lunch where they can bond and share much fun and laughter with one another while the adults engage in conversation about church service and upcoming family events

Dad prayers over the food:

Father God we thank you for the Food before us

The Family and Friends beside us

And the love between us in Jesus name we pray Amen.

9.

Having a personal family Bible study is very important for a family to have and more important for both father and mother to make time to learn about the bible together and in return teach their children about the bible scriptures and encourage one another to live and love as the bible instructs us to do.

When Victoria is a bit older she wants to sing in the children's choir

Because she loves to sing so her parents encourage her to sing for God because singing for God is a beautiful thing to do.

Dad and mom say a prayer asking God to Bless Victoria with a beautiful singing voice.

Father God in heaven please bless our daughter Victoria whom you have blessed us with talent and to be a great singer we pray that she always sings for you to be of encouragement to others all over the world in Jesus name we ask for this blessing Amen.

11.

Every Tuesday at 7 P.M. the family meets in the living room to pray and sometimes some of the neighbors who are friends with the Robinson family will attend the 7 P.M. prayer time as well and after prayer is over the family and friends may talk or watch one of their favorite television shows until it is time for everyone to go to bed.

12.

Let's always make God smile by showing and giving love to each other.

God wants all families to love and respect one another it makes him very pleased to see families getting along together,

God does not like when families fight so no matter what never fight with your family it does not make God happy.

13.

Victoria's Parents encourage her to pray every day by doing this her parents pray with her on a daily basis because talking to God and building a relationship with God and reading the Bible is very important.

14.

When Victoria and her parents travel anywhere they always pray to God and ask him for protection when they are on the road because not everyone drives safely and accidents can happen so the family wants to be protected at all times when they are driving in the car.

Dad Mom and Victoria hold hands and Dad prays:

Father God in the name of Jesus we humbly come to you and ask you to please keep us safe as we travel to and from our destination as I drive our car let me be aware of all the drivers and the traffic so that we may arrive at our destination safely and make it back home unharmed in the name of Jesus we ask these things Amen.

15.

Although Victoria is a very young child her parents realize that teaching her about God, prayer and the bible can and will make a big difference in Victoria's life as she gets older the bible is the best teacher and the only way to truly get to know God, Victoria's parents believe as they learn about God and study the bible that it is only right they share what they learn with their daughter so that she can have a happy life.

16.

Victoria and her parent prepare for bed Dad gets the bible as he does every night and the family chooses scriptures to read, tonight's bed time scriptures will be Matthew 19:13-14 and Proverbs 22:6

Matthew 13: Then people brought little children to Jesus for him to place his hands on them and pray for them. But the disciples rebuked them.

Matthew 14: Jesus said, "Let the little children come to me, and do not hinder them, for the kingdom of heaven belongs to such as these.

Proverbs 22:6

Train up a child in the way he should go, and when he is old he will not depart from it.

As Victoria lies down to rest her mother says her favorite prayer, Dad also enjoys when mom says the prayer because she says it with love and sincerity bringing peace to the families minds and hearts.

And mom begins the Prayer: Now I lay me down to sleep I pray the Lord my soul to keep. If I should die before I wake, I pray to God my soul to take if I should live for other days I pray the Lord guide my ways.

Dad then prayers for the family as well: Father unto thee I pray, thou hast guarded me all day; safe I am while in thy sight, safely let me sleep tonight bless my friends, the whole world bless; help me to learn helpfulness; keep me ever in thy sight so to all I say good night.

THE END

18.

Please reflect on some pictures of Gods Beautiful creations

19.

God is Love and he wants us to give and show love

At all times and be forgiving as well.

It is better to love than to hate

When humans are living in harmony

It pleases God.

When a child prays it brings Joy to God

Children never be ashamed to pray

God hears your prayers.

23.

The True Knowledge is found in the Bible

Learn the word and lock it in your mind and heart

And never let it go

Gods word is our food to live a safe life.

24.

Living under the care of Jesus

Is the best way to live

He will provide safety and all we need

We must be thankful for the Gift and the sacarifice that

Jesus gave to us.

25.

Unity strengthens us

So let us come together as one

And be of encouragement to one another.

www.ingramcontent.com/pod-product-compliance
Lightning Source LLC
Chambersburg PA
CBHW060801090426
42736CB00002B/119